MOTHER AND CHILD

A TREASURY OF VERSE AND PROSE
SCENTED BY PENHALIGON'S

MOTHER *and* CHILD

EDITED BY SHEILA PICKLES

HARMONY BOOKS
NEW YORK

Dedication

For my mother, Ella Maude,
hoping that her great qualities will be inherited by
my children, James and Charlotte Rose.

Contents

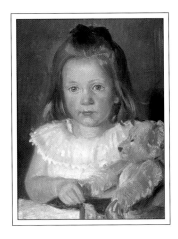

INTRODUCTION

Dear Reader,

Selecting the pieces for this anthology has been a pleasure, for many of them recall my own childhood. My earliest memories are of my mother singing "Golden Slumbers" to me in the nursery, and my sister and I can still recite the poems of A A Milne and Robert Louis Stevenson that my mother used to read to us. Sharing stories and poems with a child is wonderfully rewarding and opens the door to reading, which is a gift for life.

After such a happy childhood I was excited at the prospect of having children of my own, and it came as rather a surprise to find that little boys today are not like Christopher Robin and that my daughter's favourite poem is "A Lesson for Mamma". Being a mother has called on untried reserves of patience, and I have frequently turned to the wise words in Kahlil Gibran's *The Prophet* for guidance.

Whilst this collection is primarily about the unique relationship between mother and child, fathers are now frequently present at the birth itself and share the joy and anxiety. I have therefore included pieces which reflect the strong bond that forms between father and child as a result of this early involvement.

There is no substitute for a happy childhood in a loving family; it gives the child the base it needs for a well-balanced life, and the mother a true sense of pride and accomplishment. When my children leave home I hope they will carry with them the immortal words of Rudyard Kipling's "If", and as long as they are happy within themselves I will be satisfied.

Sheila Pickles, London, 1993

CHILDREN

And a woman who held a babe against her bosom said, Speak to us of Children.
And he said :
Your children are not your children.
They are the sons and daughters of Life's longing for itself.
They come through you but not from you,
And though they are with you yet they belong not to you.

You may give them your love but not your thoughts,
For they have their own thoughts.
You may house their bodies but not their souls,
For their souls dwell in the house of tomorrow, which you
    cannot visit, not even in your dreams.
You may strive to be like them, but seek not to make them like
    you.
For life goes not backward nor tarries with yesterday.

You are the bows from which your children as living arrows
    are sent forth.
The Archer sees the mark upon the path of the infinite, and
    He bends you with His might that His arrows may go
    swift and far.
Let your bending in the Archer's hand be for gladness ;
For even as He loves the arrow that flies, so He loves also the
    bow that is stable.

FROM *THE PROPHET* BY KAHLIL GIBRAN, 1883-1931

THE NURSERY

Our birth is but a sleep and a forgetting:
The Soul that rises with us, our life's Star

Awaiting the Birth

A LESS dismal preoccupation came to distract him – his wife's pregnancy. The nearer her time drew, the fonder husband he became. It made a new bond of the flesh between them, a constant reminder of their growing union. When he watched from a distance her indolent gait, her body turning limply on her uncorseted hips, when he feasted his eyes on her as she lounged wearily in her easy chair opposite him, his happiness overflowed: he went over and kissed her, stroked her cheek, called her "little mummy", tried to dance her round the room, and uttered between tears and laughter all manner of playful endearments that came into his head. He was overjoyed at the idea of becoming a father. Nothing was lacking to him now. He had been through the whole of human experience: serenely he settled down with both elbows firmly planted upon the table of life.

After her first feeling of astonishment Emma was eager to have the child and so find out what it felt like to be a mother.

She wanted a son. He should be dark and strong, and she would call him Georges. The thought of having a male child afforded her a kind of anticipatory revenge for all her past helplessness. A man, at any rate, is free. He can explore the passions and the continents, can surmount obstacles, reach out to the most distant joys. Whereas a woman is constantly thwarted. At once inert and pliant, she has to contend with both physical weakness and legal subordination. Her will is like the veil on her bonnet, fastened by a single string and quivering at every breeze that blows. Always there is a desire that impels and a convention that restrains.

The baby was born at about six o'clock one Sunday morning as the sun was rising.

"It's a girl," said Charles.

She turned away and fainted.

FROM *MADAME BOVARY* BY GUSTAVE FLAUBERT, 1821-1880

TO A CHILD

By what astrology of fear or hope
Dare I to cast thy horoscope!
Like the new moon thy life appears;
A little strip of silver light,
And widening outward into night
The shadowy disk of future years;
And yet upon its outer rim,
A luminous circle, faint and dim,
And scarcely visible to us here,
Rounds and completes the perfect sphere;
A prophecy and intimation,
A pale and feeble adumbration,
Of the great world of light, that lies
Behind all human destinies.

HENRY WADSWORTH LONGFELLOW. 1807-1882

MOTHERHOOD

Natásha had married in the early spring of 1813, and in 1820 already had three daughters, besides a son for whom she had longed and whom she was now nursing. She had grown stouter and broader, so that it was difficult to recognize the slim lively Natásha of former days in this robust motherly woman. Her features were more defined and had a calm, soft and serene expression. In her face there was none of the ever-glowing animation that had formerly burned there and constituted its charm. Now her face and body were often all that one saw, and her soul was not visible at all. All that struck the eye was a strong, handsome and fertile woman. The old fire very rarely kindled in her face now. That happened only when, as was the case that day, her husband returned home, or a sick child was convalescent, or on the rare occasions when something happened to induce her to sing, a practice she had quite abandoned since her marriage. At the rare moments when the old fire kindled in her handsome fully-developed body she was even more attractive than in former days.

All who had known Natásha before her marriage wondered at the change in her as at something extraordinary. Only the old countess, with her maternal instinct, had realized that all Natásha's outbursts had been due to her need of children and a husband and her mother was now surprised by the surprise expressed by those who had never understood Natásha, and kept saying that she had always known that Natásha would make an exemplary wife and mother.

"Only she lets her love of her husband and children overflow all bounds," said the countess, "so that it even becomes absurd."

FROM WAR AND PEACE BY COUNT LEO TOLSTOY, 1828-1910

ANNA'S JOY

THE weeks passed on, the time drew near, they were very gentle, and delicately happy. The insistent, passionate, dark soul, the powerful unsatisfaction in him seemed stilled and tamed, the lion lay down with the lamb in him.

She loved him very much indeed, and he waited near her. She was a precious, remote thing to him at this time, as she waited for her child. Her soul was glad with an ecstasy because of the coming infant. She wanted a boy: oh very much she wanted a boy.

But she seemed so young and so frail. She was indeed only a girl. As she stood by the fire washing herself – she was proud to wash herself at this time – and he looked at her, his heart was full of extreme tenderness for her. Such fine, fine limbs, her slim, round arms like chasing lights, and her legs so simple and childish, yet so very proud. Oh, she stood on proud legs, with a lovely reckless balance of her full belly, and the adorable little roundnesses, and the breasts becoming important. Above it all, her face was like a rosy cloud shining.

How proud she was, what a lovely proud thing her young body! And she loved him to put his hand on her ripe fulness, so that he should thrill also with the stir and the quickening there. He was afraid and silent, but she flung her arms round his neck with proud, impudent joy.

The pains came on, and Oh – how she cried! She would have him stay with her. And after her long cries she would look at him, with tears in her eyes and a sobbing laugh on her face, saying:

"I don't mind it really."

It was bad enough. But to her it was never deathly. Even the fierce, tearing pain was exhilarating. She screamed and suffered, but was all the time curiously alive and vital. She felt so powerfully alive and in the hands of such a masterly force of life, that her bottom-most feeling was one of exhilaration. She knew she was winning, winning, she was always winning, with each onset of pain she was nearer to victory.

FROM THE RAINBOW BY D H LAWRENCE. 1885-1930

LEVIN'S ORDEAL

H E did not know whether it was late or early. The candles
were all burning low. Dolly had just entered the study
and suggested that the doctor should lie down. Levin sat
listening to the doctor's stories of a quack magnetizer and
staring at the ash of the doctor's cigarette. It was an interval
of rest and oblivion. He had quite forgotten what was going
on. He listened to the doctor's tale and understood it.

Suddenly there was a scream unlike anything he had ever heard.

Quite beside himself, he rushed into her room. The screaming had ceased, and he heard a sound of movement, of rustling, of accelerated breathing, and her voice, faltering, living, tender, and happy, as it said, "It's over".

He raised his head. With her arms helplessly outstretched upon the quilt, unusually beautiful and calm she lay, gazing silently at him, trying unsuccessfully to smile.

And suddenly, out of the mysterious, terrible, and unearthly world in which he had been living for the last twenty-two hours, Levin felt himself instantaneously transported back to the old everyday world, but now radiant with the light of such new joy that it was insupportable. The taut strings snapped, and sobs and tears of joy that he had not in the least anticipated arose within him, with such force that they shook his whole body and long prevented his speaking.

Falling on his knees by her bedside he held his wife's hand to his lips, kissing it, and that hand, by a feeble movement of the fingers, replied to the kisses. And meanwhile at the foot of the bed, like a flame above a lamp, flickered in Mary Vlasevna's skilful hands the life of a human being who had never before existed : a human being who, with the same right and the same importance to himself, would live and would procreate others like himself.

"Alive! Alive! And a boy! Don't be anxious," Levin heard Mary Vlasevna say, as she slapped the baby's back with a shaking hand.

"Mama, is it true?" asked Kitty.

The Princess could only sob in reply.

And amid the silence, as a positive answer to the mother's question, a voice quite unlike all the restrained voices that had been speaking in the room made itself heard. It was a bold, insolent voice that had no consideration for anything, it was the cry of the new human being who had so incomprehensibly appeared from some unknown realm.

FROM *ANNA KARENINA* BY COUNT LEO TOLSTOY, 1828-1910

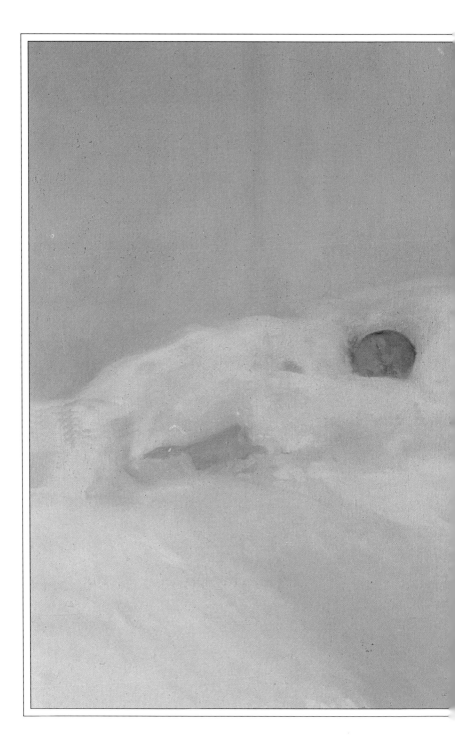

Once in Royal David's City

Once in royal David's city
   Stood a lowly cattle shed,
Where a mother laid her baby
   In a manger for his bed :
Mary was that mother mild,
Jesus Christ her little child.

He came down to earth from heaven,
   Who is God and Lord of all,
And his shelter was a stable,
   And his cradle was a stall ;
With the poor, and mean, and lowly,
Lived on earth our Saviour holy.

And through all his wondrous childhood,
   He would honour and obey,
Love and watch the lowly maiden
   In whose gentle arms he lay :
Christian children all must be
Mild, obedient, good as he.

And our eyes at last shall see him,
   Through his own redeeming love,
For that child so dear and gentle
   Is our Lord in heaven above ;
And he leads his children on
To the place where he is gone.

CECIL FRANCES ALEXANDER, 1818-1895

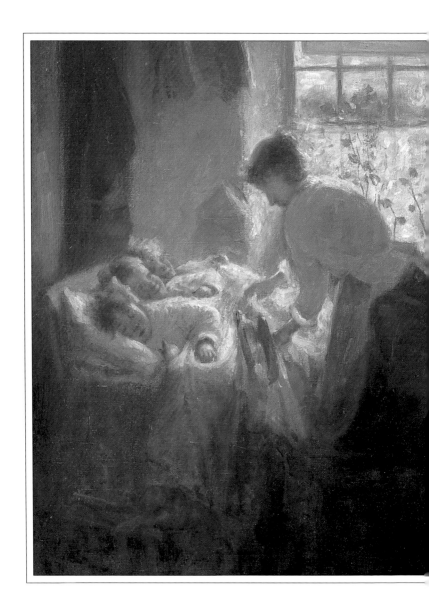

THE HAMLET BABIES

WHEN the hamlet babies arrived, they found good clothes awaiting them, and the best of all nourishment — Nature's own. The mothers did not fare so well. It was the fashion at that time to keep maternity patients on low diet for the first three days, and the hamlet women found no difficulty in following this régime; water gruel, dry toast, and weak tea was their menu. When the time came for more nourishing diet, the parson's daughter made for every patient one large sago pudding, followed up by a jug of veal broth. After these were consumed they returned to their ordinary food, with a half-pint of stout a day for those who could afford it. No milk was taken, and yet their own milk supply was abundant. Once, when a bottle-fed baby was brought on a visit to the hamlet, its bottle was held up as a curiosity. It had a long, thin rubber tube for the baby to suck through which must have been impossible to clean.

The only cash outlay in an ordinary confinement was half a crown, the fee of the old woman who, as she said, saw the beginning and end of everybody. She was, of course, not a certified midwife; but she was a decent, intelligent old body, clean in her person and methods and very kind. For the half-crown she officiated at the birth and came every morning for ten days to bath the baby and make the mother comfortable. She also tried hard to keep the patient in bed for the ten days; but with little success. Some mothers refused to stay there because they knew they were needed downstairs; others because they felt so strong and fit they saw no reason to lie there. Some women actually got up on the third day, and, as far as could be seen at the time, suffered no ill effects.

Complications at birth were rare; but in the two or three cases where they did occur during her practice, old Mrs Quinton had sufficient skill to recognize the symptoms and send post haste for the doctor. No mother lost her life in childbed during the decade.

FROM *LARK RISE TO CANDLEFORD* BY FLORA THOMPSON, 1876-1947

INFANCY

Man's breathing Miniature! thou mak'st me sigh —
A Babe art thou — and such a Thing am I!

THE ANGELS ARE STOOPING

THE angels are stooping
  Above your bed ;
They weary of trooping
With the whimpering dead.

God's laughing in Heaven
To see you so good ;
The Sailing Seven
Are gay with His mood.

I sigh that kiss you,
For I must own
That I shall miss you
When you have grown.

W B YEATS. 1865-1939

THE BABY'S DANCE
....

DANCE, little baby, dance up high,
Never mind baby, mother is by ;
Crow and caper, caper and crow,
There little baby, there you go :
Up to the ceiling, down to the ground,
Backwards and forwards, round and round.
Then dance, little baby, and mother shall sing,
With the merry gay coral, ding, ding, a-ding, ding.

ANN TAYLOR, 1782-1866

A Cradle Song

SWEET dreams form a shade,
O'er my lovely infants head.
Sweet dreams of pleasant streams.
By happy silent moony beams.

Sweet sleep with soft down,
Weave thy brows an infant crown.
Sweet sleep Angel mild,
Hover o'er my happy child.

Sweet smiles in the night,
Hover over my delight.
Sweet smiles Mothers smiles
All the livelong night beguiles.

Sweet moans, dovelike sighs,
Chase not slumber from thy eyes.
Sweet moans, sweeter smiles.
All the dovelike moans beguiles.

Sleep sleep happy child.
All creation slept and smil'd.
Sleep sleep, happy sleep.
While o'er thee thy mother weep.

WILLIAM BLAKE, 1757-1827

Intimations of Immortality

From Recollections of Early Childhood

Our birth is but a sleep and a forgetting :
  The Soul that rises with us, our life's Star,
    Hath had elsewhere its setting,
      And cometh from afar :
    Not in entire forgetfulness,
    And not in utter nakedness,
But trailing clouds of glory do we come
    From God, who is our home :
Heaven lies about us in our infancy !
Shades of the prison-house begin to close
    Upon the growing Boy,
But He beholds the light, and whence it flows,
    He sees it in his joy ;
The Youth, who daily farther from the east
    Must travel, still is Nature's Priest,
    And by the vision splendid
    Is on his way attended ;
At length the Man perceives it die away,
And fade into the light of common day.

WILLIAM WORDSWORTH, 1770-1850

GOLDEN slumbers kiss your eyes,
Smiles awake you when you rise.
Sleep, pretty wantons, do not cry,
And I will sing a lullaby :
Rock them, rock them, lullaby.

Care is heavy, therefore sleep you ;
You are care, and care must keep you.
Sleep, pretty wantons, do not cry,
And I will sing a lullaby :
Rock them, rock them, lullaby.

THOMAS DEKKER, 1572?–1632

Hester's Treasure

ONE peculiarity of the child's deportment remains yet to be told. The very first thing which she had noticed, in her life, was—what?—not the mother's smile, responding to it, as other babies do, by that faint, embryo smile of the little mouth, remembered so doubtfully afterwards, and with such fond discussion whether it were indeed a smile. By no means! But that first object of which Pearl seemed to become aware was—shall we say it?—the scarlet letter on Hester's bosom! One day, as her mother stooped over the cradle, the infant's eyes had been caught by the glimmering of the gold embroidery about the letter; and, putting up her little hand, she grasped at it, smiling, not doubtfully, but with a decided gleam that gave her face the look of a much older child. Then, gasping for breath, did Hester Prynne clutch the fatal token, instinctively endeavouring to tear it away; so infinite was the torture inflicted by the intelligent touch of Pearl's baby-hand. Again, as if her mother's agonized gesture were meant only to make sport for her, did little Pearl look into her eyes, and smile! From that epoch, except when the child was asleep, Hester had never felt a moment's safety; not a moment's calm enjoyment of her. Weeks, it is true, would sometimes elapse, during which Pearl's gaze might never once be fixed upon the scarlet letter; but then, again, it would come at unawares, like the stroke of sudden death, and always with that peculiar smile, and odd expression of the eyes.

FROM *THE SCARLET LETTER* BY NATHANIEL HAWTHORNE, 1804-1864

MATERNAL DEVOTION

"Give him to me – give him to me," said the young mother. "Give him to me, Mary," and she almost tore the child out of her sister's arms. The poor little fellow murmured somewhat at the disturbance, but nevertheless nestled himself close into his mother's bosom.

"Here, Mary, take the cloak from me. My own, own darling, darling, darling jewel. You are not false to me. Everybody else is false; everybody else is cruel. Mamma will care for nobody, nobody, nobody, but her own, own, own little man;" and she again kissed and pressed the baby, and cried till the tears ran down over the child's face.

"He is a darling – as true as gold. What would mamma do without him? Mamma would lie down and die if she had not her own Johnny Bold to give her comfort." This and much more she said of the same kind, and for a time made no other answer to Mary's inquiries.

This kind of consolation from the world's deceit is very common.

Mothers obtain it from their children, and men from their dogs. Some men even do so from their walking sticks, which is just as rational. How is it that we can take joy to ourselves in that we are not deceived by those who have not attained the art to deceive us? In a true man, if such can be found, or a true woman, much consolation may indeed be taken.

In the caresses of her child, however, Eleanor did receive consolation; and may ill befall the man who would begrudge it to her.

FROM *BARCHESTER TOWERS* BY ANTHONY TROLLOPE, 1815-1882

To an Infant

Ah, cease thy Tears and Sobs, my little Life!
  I did but snatch away the unclasped Knife :
Some safer Toy will soon arrest thine eye
And to quick Laughter change this peevish cry !
Poor Stumbler on the rocky coast of Woe,
Tutored by Pain each source of Pain to know
Alike the foodful fruit and scorching fire
Awake thy eager grasp and young desire :
Alike the Good, the Ill offend thy sight,
And rouse the stormy Sense of shrill Affright !
Untaught, yet wise ! mid all thy brief alarms
Thou closely clingest to thy Mother's arms,
Nestling thy little face in that fond breast
Whose anxious Heavings lull thee to thy rest !

Man's breathing Miniature ! thou mak'st me sigh –
A Babe art thou – and such a Thing am I !
To anger rapid and as soon appeased,
For trifles mourning and by trifles pleased,
Break Friendship's Mirror with a tetchy blow,
Yet snatch what coals of fire on Pleasure's altar glow !

SAMUEL TAYLOR COLERIDGE, 1772-1834

—42—

MAIDEN NO MORE

As the hour of eleven drew near a person watching her might have noticed that every now and then Tess's glance flitted wistfully to the brow of the hill, though she did not pause in her sheafing. On the verge of the hour the heads of a group of children, of ages ranging from six to fourteen, rose above the stubbly convexity of the hill.

The face of Tess flushed slightly, but still she did not pause.

The eldest of the comers, a girl who wore a triangular shawl, its corner draggling on the stubble, carried in her arms what at first sight seemed to be a doll, but proved to be an infant in long clothes. Another brought some lunch. The harvesters ceased working, took their provisions, and sat down against one of the shocks. Here they fell to, the men plying a stone jar freely, and passing round a cup.

Tess Durbeyfield had been one of the last to suspend her labours. She sat down at the end of the shock, her face turned somewhat away from her companions. When she had deposited herself a man in a rabbit-skin cap and with a red handkerchief tucked into his belt, held the cup of ale over the top of the shock for her to drink. But she did not accept his offer. As soon as her lunch was spread she called up the big girl her sister, and took the baby off her, who, glad to be relieved of the burden, went away to the next shock and joined the other children playing there. Tess, with a curiously stealthy yet courageous movement, and with a still rising colour, unfastened her frock and began suckling the child.

When the infant had taken its fill the young mother sat it upright in her lap, and looking into the far distance dandled it with a gloomy indifference that was almost dislike ; then all of a sudden she fell to violently kissing it some dozens of times, as if she could never leave off, the child crying at the vehemence of an onset which strangely combined passionateness with contempt.

FROM *TESS OF THE D'URBEVILLES* BY THOMAS HARDY, 1840-1928

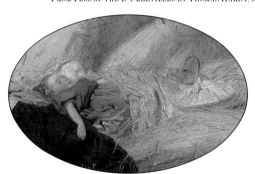

CHILDHOOD

Who dressed my doll in clothes so gay,
And fondly taught me how to play,
And minded all I had to say?
My Mother.

CHOOSING A NAME

I HAVE got a new-born sister ;
    I was nigh the first that kissed her.
When the nursing woman brought her
To papa, his infant daughter,
How papa's dear eyes did glisten ! –
She will shortly be to christen :
And papa has made the offer,
I shall have the naming of her.

Now I wonder what would please her,
Charlotte, Julia, or Louisa.
Ann and Mary, they 're too common ;
Joan 's too formal for a woman ;
Jane 's a prettier name beside ;
But we had a Jane that died.
They would say, if 'twas Rebecca,
That she was a little Quaker.
Edith 's pretty, but that looks
Better in old English books ;
Ellen 's left off long ago ;
Blanche is out of fashion now.
None that I have named as yet
Are so good as Margaret.
Emily is neat and fine.
What do you think of Caroline ?
How I 'm puzzled and perplexed
What to choose or think of next !
I am in a little fever.
Lest the name that I shall give her
Should disgrace her or defame her,
I will leave papa to name her.

CHARLES AND MARY LAMB, 1775-1834 & 1764-1847

—50—

A QUIET MOMENT

LOOKING through the window, he saw her seated in the rocking-chair with the child, already in its nightdress, sitting on her knee. The fair head with its wild, fierce hair was drooping towards the fire-warmth, which reflected on the bright cheeks and clear skin of the child, who seemed to be musing, almost like a grown-up person. The mother's face was dark and still, and he saw, with a pang, that she was away back in the life that had been. The child's hair gleamed like spun glass, her face was illuminated till it seemed like wax lit up from the inside. The wind boomed strongly. Mother and child sat motionless, silent, the child staring with vacant dark eyes into the fire, the mother looking into space. The little girl was almost asleep. It was her will which kept her eyes so wide.

Suddenly she looked round, troubled, as the wind shook the house, and Brangwen saw the small lips move. The mother began to rock, he heard the slight crunch of the rockers of the chair. Then he heard the low, monotonous murmur of a song in a foreign language. Then a great burst of wind, the mother seemed to have drifted away, the child's eyes were black and dilated. Brangwen looked up at the clouds which packed in great, alarming haste across the dark sky.

FROM *THE RAINBOW* BY D H LAWRENCE, 1885-1930

To a Child
Dancing in the Wind

Dance there upon the shore ;
    What need have you to care
For wind or water's roar ?
And tumble out your hair
That the salt drops have wet ;
Being young you have not known
The fool's triumph, nor yet
Love lost as soon as won,
Nor the best labourer dead
And all the sheaves to bind.
What need have you to dread
The monstrous crying of wind ?

W B YEATS. 1865-1939

IF NO ONE EVER MARRIES ME

IF no one ever marries me –
And I don't see why they should,
For nurse says I'm not pretty
And I'm seldom very good –

If no one ever marries me
I shan't mind very much ;
I shall buy a squirrel in a cage,
And a little rabbit hutch.

I shall have a cottage near a wood,
And a pony all my own,
And a little lamb, quite clean and tame,
That I can take to town.

And when I'm getting really old,
At twenty eight or nine,
I shall buy a little orphan girl
And bring her up as mine.

LAURENCE ALMA-TADEMA. C. 1865-1940

VESPERS

LITTLE Boy kneels at the foot of the bed,
Droops on the little hands little gold head.
Hush! Hush! Whisper who dares!
Christopher Robin is saying his prayers.

God bless Mummy. I know that's right.
Wasn't it fun in the bath tonight?
The cold's so cold, and the hot's so hot.
Oh! *God bless Daddy* – I quite forgot.

If I open my fingers a little bit more,
I can see Nanny's dressing-gown on the door.
It's a beautiful blue, but it hasn't a hood.
Oh! *God bless Nanny and make her good.*

Mine has a hood, and I lie in bed,
And pull the hood right over my head,
And I shut my eyes, and I curl up small,
And nobody knows that I'm there at all.

Oh! *Thank you, God, for a lovely day.*
And what was the other I had to say?
I said "Bless Daddy," so what can it be?
Oh, Now I remember it. *God bless Me.*

A A MILNE. 1882-1956

THE TIDE RIVER

CLEAR and cool, clear and cool,
  By laughing shallow, and dreaming pool;
Cool and clear, cool and clear,
  By shining shingle, and foaming weir;
Under the crag where the ouzel sings,
And the ivied wall where the church-bell rings,
    Undefiled, for the undefiled;
    Play by me, bathe in me, mother and child.

  Dank and foul, dank and foul,
  By the smoky town in its murky cowl;
  Foul and dank, foul and dank,
  By wharf and sewer and slimy bank;
Darker and darker the further I go,
Baser and baser the richer I grow;
    Who dare sport with the sin-defiled?
    Shrink from me, turn from me, mother and child.

CHARLES KINGSLEY, 1819-1875

MY MOTHER

Who fed me from her gentle breast,
And hushed me in her arms to rest,
And on my cheek sweet kisses prest?
    My Mother.

When pain and sickness made me cry,
Who gazed upon my heavy eye,
And wept, for fear that I should die?
    My Mother.

Who dressed my doll in clothes so gay,
And fondly taught me how to play,
And minded all I had to say?
    My Mother.

Who ran to help me when I fell,
And would some pretty story tell,
Or kiss the place to make it well?
    My Mother.

And can I ever cease to be
Affectionate and kind to thee,
Who was so very kind to me,
    My Mother?   ANN TAYLOR. 1782-1866

YOUNG NIGHT THOUGHT

ALL night long and every night,
    When my mamma puts out the light,
I see the people marching by,
As plain as day, before my eye.

Armies and emperors and kings,
All carrying different kinds of things,
And marching in so grand a way,
You never saw the like by day.
So fine a show was never seen
At the great circus on the green :
For every kind of beast and man
Is marching in that caravan.

At first they move a little slow,
But still the faster on they go,
And still beside them close I keep
Until we reach the town of Sleep.

ROBERT LOUIS STEVENSON, 1850-1894

A CHILD ABANDONED

JOYCE sat on the edge of a chair – she could not stand – watching her master with a blanched face: never had she seen him betray agitation so powerful.

"You need not mention this," he said to Joyce, indicating the note, "it concerns myself alone."

"Why – who is this?" uttered Joyce.

It was little Isabel, stealing in with a frightened face, in her white nightgown. The commotion had aroused her.

"What is the matter?" she asked. "Where's mamma?"

"Child, you'll catch your death of cold," said Joyce. "Go back to bed."

"But I want mamma."

"In the morning, dear," evasively returned Joyce. "Sir, please, must not Miss Isabel go back to bed?"

Mr. Carlyle made no reply to the question; most likely he never heard its import. But he touched Isabel's shoulder to draw Joyce's attention to the child.

"Joyce – *Miss Lucy*, in future."

He left the room, and Joyce remained silent from amazement. Isabel – nay, we must say "Lucy" also – went and stood outside the chamber door; the servants, gathered in a group near, did not observe her. Presently she came running back, and disturbed Joyce from her reverie.

"Joyce, is it true?"

"Is what true, my dear?"

"They are saying that Captain Levison has taken away mamma."

Joyce fell back in her chair, with a scream. It changed to a long, low moan of anguish.

"What has he taken her for? – to kill her? I thought it was only kidnappers who took people."

"Child, child, go to bed!"

"Oh, Joyce, I want mamma! When will she come back?"

FROM *EAST LYNNE* BY MRS HENRY WOOD, 1814-1887

Characteristics of a Child
Three Years Old

Loving she is, and tractable, though wild;
And Innocence hath privilege in her
To dignify arch looks and laughing eyes;
And feats of cunning; and the pretty round
Of trespasses, affected to provoke
Mock-chastisement and partnership in play.
And, as a faggot sparkles on the hearth,
Not less if unattended and alone
Than when both young and old sit gathered round
And take delight in its activity;
Even so this happy Creature of herself
Is all-sufficient; solitude to her
Is blithe society, who fills the air
With gladness and involuntary songs.
Light are her sallies as the tripping fawn's
Forth-startled from the fern where she lay couched;
Unthought-of, unexpected, as the stir
Of the soft breeze ruffling the meadow-flowers.
Or from before it chasing wantonly
The many-coloured images imprest
Upon the bosom of a placid lake.

WILLIAM WORDSWORTH, 1770-1850

HOW TO WRITE A LETTER

MARIA intended a letter to write,
    But could not begin (as she thought) to indite ;
So went to her mother with pencil and slate,
Containing " Dear Sister ", and also a date.

" With nothing to say, my dear girl, do not think
Of wasting your time over paper and ink ;
But certainly this is an excellent way,
To try with your slate to find something to say.

" I will give you a rule," said her mother, "my dear,
Just think for a moment your sister is here,
And what would you tell her ? Consider, and then,
Though silent your tongue, you can speak with your pen. "

ELIZABETH TURNER. 1775?-1846

OF PARENTS AND CHILDREN

THE joys of parents are secret, and so are their griefs and fears: they cannot utter the one, nor they will not utter the other. Children sweeten labours, but they make misfortunes more bitter: they increase the cares of life, but they mitigate the remembrance of death.

The difference in affection of parents towards their several children is many times unequal, and sometimes unworthy, especially in the mother. A man shall see, where there is a house full of children, one or two of the eldest respected, and the youngest made wantons; but in the midst some that are as it were forgotten, who many times nevertheless prove the best. The illiberality of parents in allowance towards their children is an harmful error; makes them base; acquaints them with shifts; makes them sort with mean company; and makes them surfeit more when they come to plenty: and therefore the proof is best, when men keep their authority towards their children, but not their purse. The Italians make little difference between children and nephews or near kinsfolks; they care not though they pass not through their own body. And in nature it is much a like matter; insomuch that we see a nephew sometimes resembleth an uncle or a kinsman more than his own parent. Let parents choose betimes the vocations and courses they mean their children should take; for then they are most flexible; and let them not too much apply themselves to the disposition of their children, as thinking they will take best to that which they have most mind to.

FRANCIS BACON, 1561-1626

THE BIRTHDAY PRESENT

"Allow me! Please wait a little, Your Excellency. I'll just look in," he said, having overtaken her. He opened a big door and vanished behind it. Anna paused and waited. "He's only just woken up," said the porter when he came out again.

Just as he spoke Anna heard the sounds of a child yawning; she recognized her son by the sound of the yawn and pictured him vividly before her.

"Let me in, let me in!" she cried, and entered at the big door. To the right of the door stood a bed on which sat the boy, his nightshirt unbuttoned, bending his little body backward, stretching himself and finishing his yawn. At the moment when his lips were closing they extended into a blissful sleepy smile, and with that smile he again fell slowly and sweetly backwards.

"Serezha!" she whispered, drawing nearer with inaudible steps.

During the time they had been parted and under the influence of that gush of love which she had felt for him of late she had always imagined him as a little fellow of four, the age when she had loved him best. Now he was not even as she had left him; he was even further removed from the four-year-old child; he had grown up more and had got thinner. What did it mean? How thin his face was! How short his hair! How long his arms! How changed since she had left him! But still it was he: the slope of the head was his, the lips were his, the soft neck and the broad shoulders.

"Serezha!" she repeated, just above the child's ear.

He raised himself again on his elbow, moved his tousled head from side to side as if seeking for something, and opened his eyes. Silently and questioningly he gazed for a few moments at his mother, who stood motionless before him; then suddenly smiling blissfully, he closed his heavy eyelids and fell once more, not backwards, but forwards into her arms.

"Serezha, my dear little boy!" she uttered, catching her breath and embracing his plump little body.

"Mama!" he muttered, wriggling about in her arms so as to touch them with different parts of his body.

Sleepily smiling with closed eyes, he moved his plump hands from the back of his bed to her shoulders, leaning against her and enveloping her in that sweet scent of sleepiness and warmth which only children possess, and began rubbing himself against her neck and shoulder.

"I knew!" he said, opening his eyes. "To-day is my birthday. I knew you would come!"

FROM *ANNA KARENINA* BY COUNT LEO TOLSTOY, 1828-1910

TABLE RULES FOR LITTLE FOLKS

IN silence I must take my seat,
    And give God thanks before I eat ;
Must for my food in patience wait,
Till I am asked to hand my plate ;
I must not scold, nor whine, nor pout,
Nor move my chair nor plate about ;
With knife, or fork, or napkin ring,
I must not play, nor must I sing.
I must not speak a useless word,
For children should be seen, not heard ;
I must not talk about my food,
Nor fret if I don't think it good ;
I must not say, "The bread is old, "
"The tea is hot, " "The coffee's cold ";
My mouth with food I must not crowd,
Nor while I'm eating speak aloud ;
Must turn my head to cough or sneeze,
And when I ask, say " If you please " ;
The tablecloth I must not spoil,
Nor with my food my fingers soil ;
Must keep my seat when I have done,
Nor round the table sport or run ;
When told to rise, then I must put
My chair away with noiseless foot ;
And lift my heart to God above,
In praise for all his wondrous love.

ANONYMOUS, C. 1858

A LESSON FOR MAMMA

DEAR Mamma, if you just could be
   A tiny little girl like me,
And I your mamma, you would see
    How nice I'd be to you.
I'd always let you have your way ;
I'd never frown at you and say,
    " You are behaving ill today,
    Such conduct will not do. "

I'd always give you jelly-cake
For breakfast, and I'd never shake
My head, and say, " You must not take
    So very large a slice. "
I'd never say, " My dear, I trust
You will not make me say you *must*
Eat up your oatmeal " ; or " The crust
    You'll find, is very nice. "

I'd never say, " Well, just a *few* ! "
I'd let you stop your lessons too ;
I'd say, " They are too hard for you,
    Poor child, to understand. "
I'd put the books and slates away ;
You shouldn't do a thing but play,
And have a party every day.
    Ah-h-h ! wouldn't that be grand !

SYDNEY DAYRE (MRS COCHRAN) FL. 1881

A LARGE FAMILY

IN the first twelve years of their marriage, children came fast into the nursery at Greshamsbury. The first that was born was a boy; and in those happy halcyon days, when the old squire was still alive, great was the joy at the birth of an heir to Greshamsbury; bonfires gleamed through the country-side, oxen were roasted whole, and the customary paraphernalia of joy usual to rich Britons on such occasions were gone through with wondrous *éclat*. But when the tenth baby, and the ninth little girl, was brought into the world, the outward show of joy was not so great.

Then other troubles came on. Some of these little girls were sickly, some very sickly. Lady Arabella had her faults, and they were such as were extremely detrimental to her husband's happiness and her own; but that of being an indifferent mother was not among them. She had worried her husband daily for years because he was not in parliament, she had worried him because he would not furnish the house in Portman Square, she had worried him because he objected to have more people every winter at Greshamsbury Park than the house would hold; but now she changed her tune and worried him because Selina coughed, because Helena was hectic, because poor Sophy's spine was weak, and Matilda's appetite was gone.

Worrying from such causes was pardonable it will be said. So it was; but the manner was hardly pardonable. Selina's cough was certainly not fairly attributable to the old-fashioned furniture in Portman Square; nor would Sophy's spine have been materially benefited by her father having a seat in parliament; and yet, to have heard Lady Arabella discussing those matters in family conclave, one would have thought that she would have expected such results.

FROM *DOCTOR THORNE* BY ANTHONY TROLLOPE. 1815-1882

G. CLAUSEN 1893.

❦❦❦

ADOLESCENCE

There was a child went forth every day,
And the first object he look'd upon, that object he became

❦❦❦

There Was a Child Went Forth

THERE was a child went forth every day,
  And the first object he look'd upon, that object he
    became,
And that object became part of him for the day or a certain
    part of the day,
Or for many years or stretching cycles of years.

The early lilacs became part of this child,
And grass and white and red morning-glories, and white and
    red clover, and the song of the phœbe-bird,
And the Third-month lambs and the sow's pink-faint litter,
    and the mare's foal and the cow's calf,
And the noisy brood of the barnyard or by the mire of the
    pondside,
And the fish suspending themselves so curiously below there,
    and the beautiful curious liquid,
And the water-plants with their graceful flat heads, all
    became part of him.
His own parents, he that had father'd him and she that had
    conceiv'd him in her womb and birth'd him,
They gave this child more of themselves than that,
They gave him afterward every day, they became part of him.

WALT WHITMAN, 1819-1892

YOUNG AND OLD

WHEN all the world is young, lad,
    And all the trees are green ;
And every goose a swan, lad,
    And every lass a queen ;
Then hey for boot and horse, lad,
    And round the world away ;
Young blood must have its course, lad,
    And every dog his day.

When all the world is old, lad,
    And all the trees are brown ;
When all the sport is stale, lad,
    And all the wheels run down ;
Creep home, and take your place there,
    The spent and maimed among :
God grant you find one face there,
    You loved when all was young.

CHARLES KINGSLEY, 1819-1875

Growing Up

O^H, but she never wanted James to grow a day older or Cam either. These two she would have liked to keep for ever just as they were, demons of wickedness, angels of delight, never to see them grow up into long-legged monsters. Nothing made up for the loss. When she read just now to James, "and there were numbers of soldiers with kettle-drums and trumpets", and his eyes darkened, she thought, why should they grow up, and lose all that? He was the most gifted, the most sensitive of her children. But all, she thought, were full of promise. Prue, a perfect angel with the others , and sometimes now, at night especially, she took one's breath away with her beauty. Andrew – even her husband admitted that his gift for mathematics was extraordinary. And Nancy and Roger, they were both wild creatures now, scampering about over the country all day long. As for Rose, her mouth was too big, but she had a wonderful gift with her hands. If they had charades, Rose made the dresses; made everything; liked best arranging tables, flowers, anything. She did not like it that Jasper should shoot birds; but it was only a stage; they all went through stages. Why, she asked, pressing her chin on James's head, should they grow up so fast? Why should they go to school? She would have liked always to have had a baby. She was happiest carrying one in her arms. Then people might say she was tyrannical, domineering, masterful, if they chose; she did not mind. And, touching his hair with her lips, she thought, he will never be so happy again, but stopped herself, remembering how it angered her husband that she should say that. Still, it was true. They were happier now than they would ever be again.

FROM TO THE LIGHTHOUSE BY VIRGINIA WOOLF, 1882-1941

IF . . .

IF you can keep your head when all about you
    Are losing theirs and blaming it on you,
If you can trust yourself when all men doubt you,
    But make allowance for their doubting too ;
If you can wait and not be tired by waiting,
    Or being lied about, don't deal in lies,
Or being hated, don't give way to hating,
    And yet don't look too good, nor walk too wise :

If you can dream – and not make dreams your master ;
    If you can think – and not make thoughts your aim ;
If you can meet with Triumph and Disaster
    And treat those two impostors just the same ;
If you can bear to hear the truth you've spoken
    Twisted by knaves to make a trap for fools,
Or watch the things you gave your life to, broken,
    And stoop and build 'em up with worn-out tools :

If you can talk with crowds and keep your virtue,
    Or walk with Kings – nor lose the common touch,
If neither foes nor loving friends can hurt you,
    If all men count with you, but none too much ;
If you can fill the unforgiving minute
    With sixty seconds' worth of distance run,
Yours is the Earth and everything that's in it,
    And – which is more – you'll be a Man, my son !

RUDYARD KIPLING, 1865-1936

Boarding School

WELLS turned to the other fellows and said :
– O, I say, here's a fellow says he kisses his mother every night before he goes to bed.

The other fellows stopped their game and turned round, laughing. Stephen blushed under their eyes and said :

– I do not.

Wells said :

– O, I say, here's a fellow says he doesn't kiss his mother before he goes to bed.

They all laughed again. Stephen tried to laugh with them. He felt his whole body hot and confused in a moment. What was the right answer to the question ? He had given two and still Wells laughed. But Wells must know the right answer for he was in third of grammar. He did not like Wells's face. It was Wells who had shouldered him into the square ditch the day before because he would not swop his little snuffbox for Wells's seasoned hacking chestnut, the conqueror of forty. It was a mean thing to do ; all the fellows said it was. And how cold and slimy the water had been ! And a fellow had once seen a big rat jump plop into the scum.

The cold slime of the ditch covered his whole body ; and, when the bell rang for study and the lines filed out of the playrooms, he felt the cold air of the corridor inside his clothes. He still tried to think what was the right answer. Was it right to kiss his mother or wrong to kiss his mother ? What did that mean, to kiss ? You put your face up like that to say goodnight and then his mother put her face down. That was to kiss. His mother put her lips on his cheek ; her lips were soft and they wetted his cheek ; and they made a tiny little noise : kiss. Why did people do that with their two faces ?

Sitting in the studyhall he opened the lid of his desk and changed the number pasted up inside from seventyseven to seventysix. But the Christmas vacation was very far away ; but one time it would come because the earth moved round always.

FROM *A PORTRAIT OF THE ARTIST AS A YOUNG MAN* BY JAMES JOYCE, 1882-1941

NANNY'S PROBLEMS

"COME along now, you've had quite enough of horses for one day."

"Can't have enough of horses," said John, "ever." On the way back to the house he said, "Can I have my milk in mummy's room?"

"That depends."

Nanny's replies were always evasive, like that.

"What does it depend on?"

"Lots of things."

"Tell me one of them."

"On your not asking a lot of silly questions."

"Silly old tart."

"*John*! How dare you? What do you mean?"

Delighted by the effect of this sally, John broke away from her hand and danced in front of her, saying, "Silly old tart, silly old tart" all the way to the side entrance. When they entered the porch his nurse silently took off his leggings; he was sobered a little by her grimness.

"Go straight up to the nursery," she said. "I am going to speak to your mother about you."

"Please, nanny. I don't know what it means, but I didn't mean it."

"Go straight to the nursery."

Brenda was doing her face.

"It's been the same ever since Ben Hacket started teaching him to ride, my lady, there's been no doing anything with him."

Brenda spat in the eye-black. "But, nanny, what exactly did he say?"

"Oh, I couldn't repeat it, my lady."

"Nonsense, you must tell me. Otherwise I shall be thinking it something far worse than it was."

"It couldn't have been worse . . . he called me a silly old tart, my lady."

Brenda choked slightly into her face towel.

FROM *A HANDFUL OF DUST* BY EVELYN WAUGH, 1903-1966

The New Mamma

Mr Gibson sat down in the arm-chair made ready for him, and warmed his hands at the fire, seeming neither to need food nor talk, as he went over a train of recollections. Then he roused himself from his sadness, and looking round the room, he said briskly enough :

"And where's the new mamma ? "

"She was tired, and went to bed early. Oh, papa! Must I call her 'mamma'? "

"I should like it," replied he, with a slight contraction of the brows.

Molly was silent. She put a cup of tea near him ; he stirred it, and sipped it, and then he recurred to the subject.

"Why shouldn't you call her 'mamma'? I'm sure she means to do the duty of a mother to you. We all may make mistakes, and her ways may not be quite all at once our ways ; but at any rate let us start with a family bond between us. "

Molly had always spoken of her father's new wife as Mrs Gibson, and had once burst out at Miss Brownings' with a protestation that she never would call her "mamma". She did not feel drawn to her new relation by their intercourse that evening. She kept silence, though she knew her father was expecting an answer. At last he gave up his expectation, and turned to another subject ; but there was a certain hardness and constraint in his manner, and in hers a heaviness and absence of mind. All at once she said :

"Papa, I will call her 'mamma'! "

He took her hand, and grasped it tight ; but for an instant or two he did not speak. Then he said :

"You won't be sorry for it, Molly. "

From *Wives and Daughters* by Elizabeth Gaskell. 1810-1865

THOUGHTS OF MARRIAGE

LADY C. Marry, that "marry" is the very theme
I came to talk of. Tell me, daughter Juliet,
How stands your dispositions to be married?
JUL. It is an honour that I dream not of.
NURSE. An honour! Were not I thine only nurse,
I would say thou hadst suck'd wisdom from thy teat.
LADY C. Well, think of marriage now.
Younger than you,
Here in Verona, ladies of esteem,
Are made already mothers. By my count,
I was your mother much upon these years
That you are now a maid. Thus, then, in brief:
The valiant Paris seeks you for his love.
NURSE. A man, young lady! lady, such a man
As all the world – why, he's a man of wax.
LADY C. Verona's summer hath not such a flower.
NURSE. Nay, he's a flower; in faith, a very flower.
LADY C. What say you? Can you love the gentleman?
This night you shall behold him at our feast;
Read o'er the volume of young Paris' face,
And find delight writ there with beauty's pen;
Examine every married lineament,
And see how one another lends content;
And what obscur'd in this fair volume lies
Find written in the margent of his eyes.
This precious book of love, this unbound lover,
To beautify him, only lacks a cover.
This fish lives in the sea, and 'tis much pride
For fair without the fair within to hide.
That book in many's eyes doth share the glory
That in gold clasps locks in the golden story;
So shall you share all that he doth possess,
By having him making yourself no less.
NURSE. No less! Nay, bigger; women grow by men.
LADY C. Speak briefly, can you like of Paris' love?
JUL. I'll look to like, if looking liking move;
But no more deep will I endart mine eye
Than your consent gives strength to make it fly.

FROM *ROMEO AND JULIET* BY WILLIAM SHAKESPEARE, 1564-1616

A Confrontation in the Kitchen

Sophia was not a good child, and she obstinately denied in her heart the cardinal principle of family life, namely, that the parent has conferred on the offspring a supreme favour by bringing it into the world. She interrupted her mother again, rudely.

"I don't want to leave school at all," she said passionately.

"But you will have to leave school sooner or later," argued Mrs Baines, with an air of quiet reasoning, of putting herself on a level with Sophia. "You can't stay at school for ever, my pet, can you? Out of my way!"

She hurried across the kitchen with a pie, which she whipped into the oven, shutting the iron door with a careful gesture.

"Yes," said Sophia. "I should like to be a teacher. That's what I want to be."

"A school-teacher?" inquired Mrs Baines.

"Of course. What other kind is there?" said Sophia, sharply.

"I don't think your father would like that," Mrs Baines replied. "I'm sure he wouldn't like it."

"Why not?"

"It wouldn't be quite suitable."

"Why not, mother?" the girl demanded with a sort of ferocity. She had now quitted the range.

Mrs Baines was startled and surprised. Sophia's attitude was really very trying; her manners deserved correction.

The experience of being Sophia's mother for nearly sixteen years had not been lost on Mrs Baines, and though she was now discovering undreamt-of dangers in Sophia's erratic temperament, she kept her presence of mind sufficiently well to behave with diplomatic smoothness. It was undoubtedly humiliating to a mother to be forced to use diplomacy in dealing with a girl in short sleeves. In *her* day mothers had been autocrats. But Sophia was Sophia.

FROM *The Old Wives' Tale* by Arnold Bennett, 1867-1931

My Boy Jack

"Have you news of my boy Jack?"
   Not this tide.
"When d'you think that he'll come back?"
   Not with this wind blowing, and this tide.

"Has any one else had word of him?"
   Not this tide.
For what is sunk will hardly swim,
   Not with this wind blowing, and this tide.

"Oh, dear, what comfort can I find!"
   None this tide,
   Nor any tide,
Except he did not shame his kind –
   Not even with that wind blowing, and that tide.

Then hold your head up all the more,
   This tide,
   And every tide;
Because he was the son you bore,
   And gave to that wind blowing and that tide!

RUDYARD KIPLING, 1865-1936

MOTHER O' MINE

(DEDICATION TO "THE LIGHT THAT FAILED")

IF I were hanged on the highest hill,
   Mother o' mine, O mother o' mine!
I know whose love would follow me still,
Mother o' mine, O mother o' mine!

If I were drowned in the deepest sea,
Mother o' mine, O mother o' mine!
I know whose tears would come down to me,
Mother o' mine, O mother o' mine!

If I were damned of body and soul,
I know whose prayer would make me whole,
Mother o' mine, O mother o' mine!

RUDYARD KIPLING, 1865-1936

MRS WARREN'S AGONY

VIVIE. I am my mother's daughter. I am like you: I must
have work, and must make more money than I spend. But my
work is not your work, and my way not your way. We must
part. It will not make much difference to us: instead of
meeting one another for perhaps a few months in twenty
years, we shall never meet: that's all.

MRS WARREN *(her voice stifled in tears)* Vivie: I meant to
have been more with you: I did indeed.

VIVIE. It's no use, mother: I am not to be changed by a few
cheap tears and entreaties any more than you are, I dare say.

MRS WARREN *(wildly)* Oh, you call a mother's tears cheap.

VIVIE. They cost you nothing; and you ask me to give you the
peace and quietness of my whole life in exchange for them.
What use would my company be to you if you could get it?
What have we two in common that could make either of us
happy together?

MRS WARREN *(lapsing recklessly into her dialect)* We're
mother and daughter. I want my daughter. I've a right to
you. Who is to care for me when I'm old? Plenty of girls have
taken to me like daughters and cried at leaving me; but I let
them all go because I had you to look forward to. I kept
myself lonely for you. You've no right to turn on me now and
refuse to do your duty as a daughter.

VIVIE *(jarred and antagonized by the echo of the slums in her
mother's voice)* My duty as a daughter! I thought we should
come to that presently. Now once for all, mother, you want a
daughter and Frank wants a wife. I don't want a mother;
and I don't want a husband. I have spared neither Frank nor
myself in sending him about his business. Do you think I will
spare you?

FROM *MRS WARREN'S PROFESSION* BY GEORGE BERNARD SHAW, 1856-1950

EQUALITY

"*APROPOS de Varenka*," said Kitty in French, which they had been speaking all the time so that Agatha Mikhaylovna should not understand them. "Do you know, Mama, I am somehow expecting it to be settled to-day! You understand what I mean. How nice it would be!"

"Dear me! What a skilful matchmaker!" teased Dolly. "How carefully and adroitly she brings them together!"

"Come, Mama! Tell me what you think about it?"

"What am I to think? He" (*he* meant Koznyshev) "could have made the best match in Russia any time; now he is no longer so young, but all the same I am sure many would marry him even now. . . . She is very good-natured, but he might . . ."

"Oh, but, Mama, try and understand why nothing better could be imagined either for him or for her. First of all, she is simply charming!" expostulated Kitty, crooking one finger.

"He certainly likes her very much," Dolly chimed in.

"Secondly, his position in the world is such that neither property nor the social position of his wife matters to him at all. He only needs a good, sweet, quiet wife."

"Yes, one certainly can trust her," again chimed in Dolly.

"Thirdly, she must love him; and that too is . . . In a word, it would be splendid! I expect when they come back from the wood it will all be settled. I shall see it at once by their eyes. I should be so glad! What do you think, Dolly?"

"But don't get excited; there is no need at all for you to get excited," admonished her mother.

"But I am not excited, Mama! I think he will propose to-day."

"Ah, how strange it is when and how a man proposes. . . . There is a sort of barrier, and suddenly down it goes," said Dolly with a dreamy smile, recalling her past with Oblonsky.

"Mama, how did Papa propose to you?" Kitty suddenly inquired.

"There was nothing special about it – it was quite simple,"

answered the Princess, but her face brightened at the memory.

"No, but how . . . ? You really loved him before you were allowed to talk to one another?"

Kitty felt a particular charm in being able now to talk with her mother as an equal about those chief events in a woman's life.

FROM *ANNA KARENINA* BY COUNT LEO TOLSTOY, 1828-1910

THE REUNION

I SAID some very tender, kind things in the letter about his
son, which I told him he knew to be my own child, and I
hoped he would allow me the most passionate desire of once
seeing my own and only child.

I did believe that, having received this letter, he would
immediately give it to his son to read, his eyes being, I knew,
so dim that he could not see to read it; but it fell out better
than so, for my letter came directly to my son's hand, and he
opened and read it.

He called the messenger in, after some little stay, and
asked him where the person was who gave him that letter. Let
any one judge the consternation I was in when my messenger
came back and told me the old gentleman was not at home,
but his son was come along with him, and was just coming up
to me. I was perfectly confounded, for I knew not whether it
was peace or war, nor could I tell how to behave; however, I
had but a very few moments to think, for my son was at the
heels of the messenger, and coming up into my lodgings,
asked the fellow at the door something. I suppose it was, for I
did not hear it, which was the gentlewoman that sent him; for
the messenger said, "There she is, sir"; at which he comes
directly up to me, kisses me, took me in his arms, embraced
me with so much passion that he could not speak, but I could

feel his breast heave and throb like a child, that cries, but sobs, and cannot cry out.

I can neither express or describe the joy that touched my very soul when I found, for it was easy to discover that part, that he came not as a stranger, but as a son to a mother, and indeed a son who had never before known what a mother of his own was; in short, we cried over one another a considerable while, when at last he broke out first. "My dear mother," says he, "are you still alive? I never expected to have seen your face." As for me, I could say nothing a great while.

FROM *MOLL FLANDERS* BY DANIEL DEFOE, 1661-1731

The Ultimatum

SHE would not give him time to reply, but hurrying instantly to her husband, called out as she entered the library,

"Oh! Mr Bennet; you are wanted immediately; we are all in an uproar. You must come and make Lizzy marry Mr Collins, for she vows she will not have him, and if you do not make haste he will change his mind and not have *her.*"

Mr Bennet raised his eyes from his book as she entered, and fixed them on her face with a calm unconcern which was not in the least altered by her communication.

"I have not the pleasure of understanding you," said he, when she had finished her speech. "Of what are you talking?"

"Of Mr Collins and Lizzy. Lizzy declares she will not have Mr Collins, and Mr Collins begins to say that he will not have Lizzy."

"And what am I to do on the occasion? – It seems an hopeless business."

"Speak to Lizzy about it yourself. Tell her that you insist upon her marrying him."

"Let her be called down. She shall hear my opinion."

Mrs Bennet rang the bell, and Miss Elizabeth was summoned to the library.

"Come here, child," cried her father as she appeared. "I have sent for you on an affair of importance. I understand that Mr Collins has made you an offer of marriage. Is it true?" Elizabeth replied that it was. "Very well – and this offer of marriage you have refused?"

"I have, sir."

"Very well. We now come to the point. Your mother insists upon your accepting it. Is not it so, Mrs Bennet?"

"Yes, or I will never see her again."

"An unhappy alternative is before you, Elizabeth. From this day you must be a stranger to one of your parents. Your mother will never see you again if you do *not* marry Mr Collins, and I will never see you again if you *do.*"

FROM *PRIDE AND PREJUDICE* BY JANE AUSTEN, 1775-1817

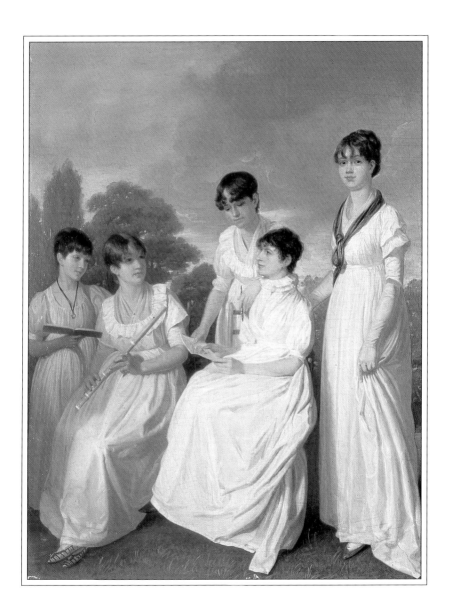

TO ANY READER

As from the house your mother sees
You playing round the garden trees,
So you may see, if you will look
Through the windows of this book,
Another child, far, far away,
And in another garden, play.
But do not think you can at all,
By knocking on the window, call
That child to hear you. He intent
Is all on his play-business bent.

He does not hear ; he will not look,
Nor yet be lured out of this book.
For, long ago, the truth to say,
He has grown up and gone away,
And it is but a child of air
That lingers in the garden there.

ROBERT LOUIS STEVENSON, 1850-1894

PENHALIGON'S LILY OF THE VALLEY

I have selected the delicate Lily of the Valley to scent the endpapers of this book. The flowers can be found in shady areas in early May, and the clean green scent that comes from the tiny white bells seems appropriate to illustrate the purity of the relationship between mother and child.

Sheila Pickles

ACKNOWLEDGEMENTS

PICTURE CREDITS:

Bridgeman Art Library, London:
p1 *Mrs Winston Churchill and her Daughter Sarah*: Sir John Lavery/Roy Miles
Fine Paintings, London; p2 *Out of Reach, The Daughters of Eve*: Sir Frank
Dicksee/Chris Beetles Ltd, London; p6/7 *Roses and Lilies*: Mary Louise
Maemonnies/Musée des Beaux Arts, Rouen/Photographie Giraudon, Paris; p9 *The
Three Sisters*: Johann Georg Meyer von Bremen/Josef Mensing Gallery, Hamm-
Rhynern; p10/11 *Motherhood*: Louis Emile Adan/Waterhouse & Dodd, London;
p12 *La Pensée*: Pierre Auguste Renoir/National Gallery of Art, Washington; p15
The Astrologer: Sir Edward Burne-Jones/Agnew & Sons, London; p18 *Alfred
Sisley* (detail): Pierre Auguste Renoir/Art Institute of Chicago; p19 *Après le
Bain, Femme S'essuyant les Pieds*: Edgar Degas/Musée d'Orsay/Photographie
Giraudon, Paris; p20 *Portrait of Auguste Renoir*: Frederic Bazille/Musée
d'Orsay/Photographie Giraudon, Paris; p22/23 *Mother, 1895*: Joaquin y Bastida
Sorolla/Museo Sorolla, Madrid; p25 *Madonna with the Iris*: Albrecht Durer/
National Gallery, London; p28/29 *Mother and Child*: William-Adolph Bouguerea/
Private Collection; p30 *Le Berceau*: Berthe Morisot/Louvre, Paris; p32/33 *Day
Dreams*: Walter Langley/City of Bristol Museum and Art Gallery; p39 *Mother
and Child*: Wilfred Fairclough/Warrington Museum and Art Gallery; p41
Maternal Love: Vincenzo Irolli/Josef Mensing Gallery, Hamm-Rhynern; p42
Pontus (detail): Carl Larsson/National Museum, Stockholm; p44/45 *Promenade
des Enfants*: Timoleon Marie Lobrichon/Roy Miles Fine Paintings, London; p46
The Gleaners: Alexander Hann/Fine Art Society, London; p47 *An Afternoon Nap*
(detail): George Elgar Hicks/Agnew & Sons, London; p48/49 *Happy Family*:
André Henri Dargelas/Wolverhampton Art Gallery, Staffs; p55 *Sur la Plage*
(detail): Charles C J Hoffbauer/Musée de Roubaix/Photographie Giraudon,
Paris; p56 *A Morning Stroll*: Dorothea Sharp/Whitford & Hughes, London; p57
Going to Bed: John Burgess/Gavin Graham Gallery, London; p61 *Quiet*: W W
Nichol/York City Art Gallery; p64 *Master Baddeley of Derby with his Dog*: Otto
Leyde/Gavin Graham Gallery, London; p65 *Portrait of Lillie Langtry* (detail);
Valentine Cameron Prinsep/Christie's, London; p67 *An Impromptu Ball*: Eva
Roos/Christie's, London; p68 *An Invitation*: Mary Gow/Christopher Wood
Gallery, London; p71 *Portrait of a Family Group*, c. 1630: attributed to Cornelis
de Vos/Historical Portraits Ltd, London; p73 *Storytime*: William Oliver/Phillips,
The International Fine Art Auctioneers; p75 *Le Déjeuner*: Claude Monet/
Stadtische Galerie, Stadelsches Kunstinstitut, Frankfurt; p76/77 *The Music
Lesson*: Frederick, Lord Leighton/Guildhall Art Gallery, London; p79 *The
Daughters of Colonel Makin MP*: John Collier/Christopher Wood Gallery,
London; p80/81 *The Little Flowers of the Field*: Sir George Clausen/Private
Collection; p82 *Musing on the Future*: George Smith/Christopher Wood Gallery,
London; p83 *The Departure of the Prodigal Son*: James Jacques Tissot/Fine Art
Society, London; p85 *Little Timidity*: Frederick Samuel Beaumont/The Maas
Gallery, London; p86/87 *Boys Netting Crabs*: John Bulloch Souter/Roy Miles Fine
Paintings, London; p88 *The Meeting*: Maria Bashkirtseff/Musée d'Orsay, Paris;
p90 *The Black Hat* (detail): Francis Campbell Boileau/City of Edinburgh
Museums and Art Galleries; p93 *Sir Alexander Don with his Daughter Elizabeth*:
Sir Henry Raeburn/Christie's, London; p94 *Portrait of a Girl*: Domenico
Ghirlandaio/National Gallery, London; p97 *Portrait of a Young Woman said to be
Miss Clare Davies*: Archibald James Stuart Wortley/Phillips, The International
Fine Art Auctioneers; p98 *Portrait of the Artist's Son* (detail): Augustus
John/The Fine Art Society, London; p99 *Madame Monet on the Sofa*: Claude
Monet/Musée d'Orsay, Paris; p101 *Miss Christian Elspeth Mallock*: Edward
Arthur Walton/Private Collection; p103 *The Misses Vickers*: John Singer
Sargent/Sheffield City Art Galleries; p104 *Philip, 5th Earl of Pembroke* (detail):

Sir Anthony van Dyck/Wilton House, Wiltshire ; p105 *Portrait of a Lady* : Gabriel
Metsu/Agnew & Sons, London ; p107 *Portrait of a Mother and her Four
Daughters* : Sir George Hayter/Phillips, The International Fine Art Auctioneers.

David Messum :
p26 *Bairnies Cuddle Doon* : Robert Gemmel Hutchinson.

Fine Art Photographic Archive, London :
p3 *A Frolic* : Isaac Snowman ; p4 *A Portrait of a Young Boy* (detail) : Johan
Vilhelm Gertner ; p5 *Teddy's Company* (detail) : Michael-Peter Ancher ; p31
Bathtime : Alfred Edward Emslie ; p43 *In Disgrace* : Charles Burton Barber ; p51
Rockabye Baby : Jane M Dealey ; p54 *A Little Girl on Skagen Beach at Sunset* :
Peder Severin Kroyer ; p69 *Posting a Letter* : Albert Ludovici Jnr. ; p91 *A
Morning Ride* : Ralph Peacock.

Manchester City Art Galleries :
p35 *Christening Sunday* : James Charles.

Metropolitan Museum of Art, NY :
p108 *Jungle Tales* : James Shannon/Arthur Hoppock Hearn Fund, 1913.

Museum of Fine Arts, Boston :
p58/59 *Mother and Child in a Boat* : Edmund Charles Tarbell/Bequest of David P
Kimball in memory of his wife, Clara Bertram Kimball.

Pennsylvania Academy of the Fine Arts, Philadelphia :
p52/53 *Les Derniers Jours de l'Enfance* : Gift of Cecilia Drinker Saltonstall.

Tate Gallery, London :
p36/37 *The Cholmondeley Sisters* : British School, 17th cent.

Tunbridge Wells Museum and Art Gallery :
p17 *A Letter from Papa* : Frederick Goodall.

Wharfedale Galleries :
p62/63 *Peter Pan's Party* : Percy Tarrant/By Kind Co-operation of Medici Society,
London.

Cover : *The Artist's Wife and her Two Daughters* : H D Pagett/Christopher Wood
Gallery, London/The Bridgeman Art Library.

TEXT ACKNOWLEDGEMENTS

The following extracts were reproduced by kind permission of the following
publishers, copyright holders and agents.

p27 Extract from *Lark Rise to Candleford* by Flora Thompson, 1945, by
permission of Oxford University Press.

p57 'Vespers' from *When We Were Very Young* by A A Milne, reproduced in the
UK by permission of the publishers, Methuen Children's Books. Copyright 1924 by
E P Dutton, copyright renewed 1952 by A A Milne. Used by permission of
Dutton's Children's Books, a division of Penguin Books USA Inc.

p84 Extract from *To the Lighthouse* by Virginia Woolf, reproduced by permission
of the publishers, The Hogarth Press, and the Estate of Virginia Woolf.

p89 Extract from *A Portrait of the Artist as a Young Man* by James Joyce,
reproduced by permission of the publishers, Jonathan Cape, and the Estate of
James Joyce.

p90-1 *A Handful of Dust* by Evelyn Waugh. Reprinted by permission of the Peters
Fraser & Dunlop Group Ltd.

p100 Extract from *Mrs Warren's Profession* by George Bernard Shaw.
Reproduced by permission of the Society of Authors on behalf of the Bernard
Shaw Estate.

Published by Harmony Books,
a division of Crown Publishers, Inc.,
201 East 50th Street, New York, New York 10022.
Member of the Crown Publishing Group.
Random House, Inc. New York, Toronto, London, Sydney, Auckland.

Originally published in Great Britain by
Pavilion Books Limited in 1993.

Harmony and colophon are trademarks of
Crown Publishers Inc.

Manufactured in Hong Kong by Imago

Library of Congress Catalog Card Number : 92-54575

ISBN 0-517-59419-6

10 9 8 7 6 5 4 3 2 1

First American edition

For more information about Penhaligon's perfumes,
please telephone London 011-44-81-880-2050, or write to :
PENHALIGON'S
41 Wellington Street
Covent Garden
London WC2